A Kid's Guide to Drawing™

How to Draw
Airplanes

Laura Murawski

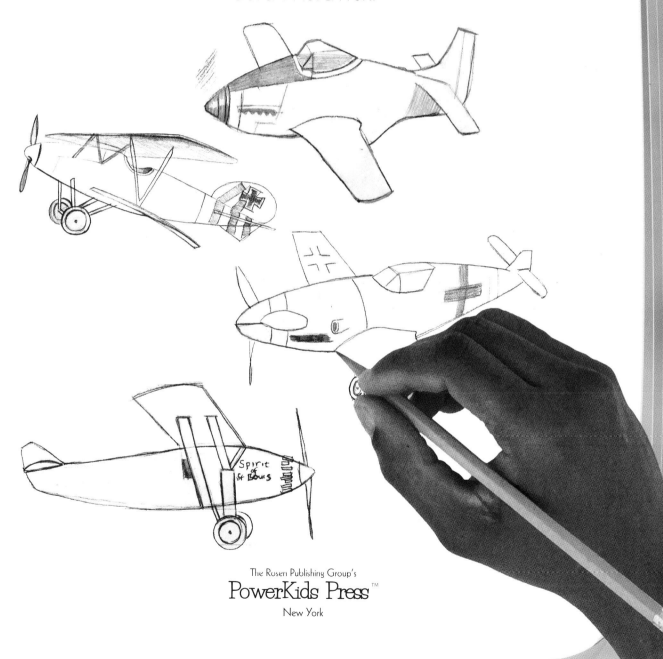

The Rosen Publishing Group's
PowerKids Press™
New York

Published in 2001 by The Rosen Publishing Group, Inc.
29 East 21st Street, New York, NY 10010

First Edition

Book Design: Kim Sonsky

Illustration Credits: Laura Murawski

Photo Credits: Title page (hand) by Arlan Dean; p. 6 © Bettmann/Corbis; p. 8 © Corbis-Bettmann; p. 10 © Richard T. Nowitz/Corbis; p. 12 © Museum of Flight/Corbis; p. 14 © George Hall/Corbis; p. 16 © Neil Rabinowitz/Corbis; p. 18 © Marc Garanger/Corbis; p. 20 © Aero Graphics, Inc./Corbis.

Murawski, Laura.
    How to draw airplanes by Laura Murawski
        p. cm. — (A kid's guide to drawing)
    Summary: Describes how to draw various airplanes, including the Wright Flyer,
Spirit of St. Louis, and Stealth Bomber.
    ISBN 0-8239-5547-8 (lib. bdg. : alk. paper)
    1. Airplanes in art—Juvenile literature. 2. Drawing—Technique—Juvenile literature.
        [1. Airplanes in art. 2. Drawing—Technique.] I. Title. II. Series.

NC825.A4 M87 2000
743'.8962913334—dc21   99-056950

Manufactured in the United States of America

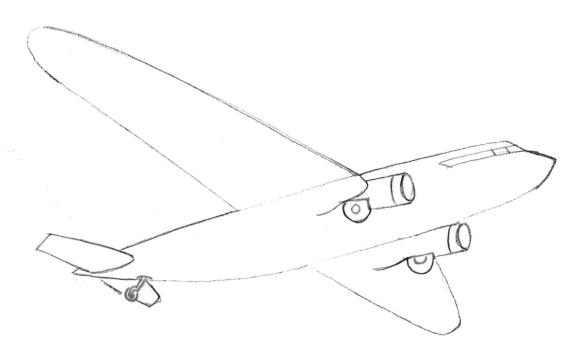

CONTENTS

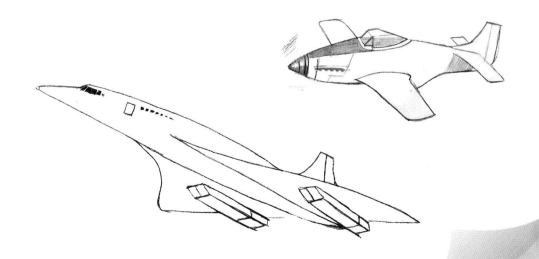

Taking Off

In this book you will learn how to draw airplanes. You will discover that it is not hard, and that it is fun!

Have you ever dreamed about flying? Have you wished that you could soar like a bird? Some people did more than just dream of flying. They invented machines called airplanes that could help lift them into the air. There are many different types of airplanes. They all have the same basic parts, such as a **nose**, **propeller**, **engine**, **cockpit**, **wings**, and **rudder**. Each type of plane also has special features that make it look different from other planes. In this book, you will learn about eight types of airplanes and how to draw them.

You will need the following supplies to draw airplanes:
- A sketch pad
- A number 2 pencil
- A pencil sharpener
- An eraser

Drawing airplanes is a lot easier than you might think. The basic shapes you use to draw airplanes are a <u>3-D box</u>, <u>rectangle</u>, <u>circle</u>, and <u>oval</u>. You will learn some new words while you are going through the easy steps of drawing airplanes. These include such words as <u>horizontal</u> and <u>vertical</u>. You can find these words and illustrations to show what they mean in a section called Drawing Terms on page 22.

The first airplane you will learn about is the *Wright Flyer*. It was the first airplane to fly, and you will learn how to draw it in six steps. There are directions under each drawing to help you through the steps. Each new step of your drawing is shown in color to help guide you.

To draw airplanes, follow the four Ps: **Patience**, **Persistence**, Practice, and a Positive **attitude**. The more you draw, the better you will become at drawing. Before you start, make sure to find a quiet, clean, and well-lit space where you can pay attention to your drawing. Good luck, and most important, have fun! Now sharpen your pencils, and let's take off!

The Wright Flyer

On December 17, 1903, two brothers, Orville and Wilbur Wright, made the first airplane flight in history. They solved the mystery of how to travel by air. They took off and landed a total of four times that day. On the longest try, Wilbur flew the *Flyer* 852 feet (260 m) in 59 seconds! The *Flyer* had 8-foot (2.4-m) propellers, which were attached to the engine with bicycle chains. The wings of the airplane were supported by pieces of wood. The rudder, at the tail of the *Flyer*, helped steer it. The front panels, called the **elevator**, moved up and down to raise and lower the front of the *Flyer*.

1

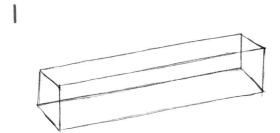

First, draw the shape of a <u>3-D box.</u>

4

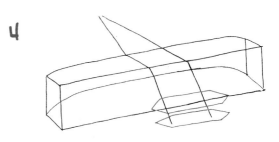

Next, add two pointed shapes at the front of the box. These shapes will form the elevator. Notice how these shapes are near the bottom of the box (bottom wing).

2

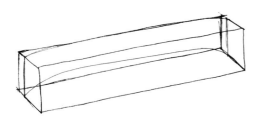

Next, curve the corners of the top and bottom sides of the box. Notice that only the corners at the back of the box are curved. You have just made the top and bottom wings!

5

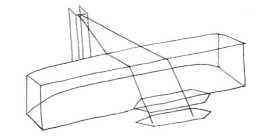

Now, to add the rudder, draw four <u>vertical</u> lines behind the box (wings). Connect these lines with three short lines.

3

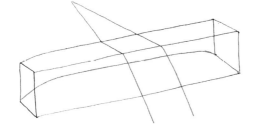

Draw a shape in the form of a <u>triangle</u> on top of the box (or wing). Continue the two lines that are the sides of the triangle. They should go across the top of the box and end just past the bottom of the box (or wings).

6

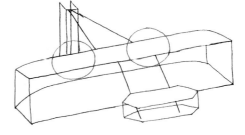

Next, draw two <u>circles</u> to make the propellers look like they are in motion. Notice how the bottom of the circles touch the bottom curved line of the box (bottom wing). Erase any extra lines.

The Albatros D. Va

The *Albatros D. Va* was a popular airplane in Germany during World War I (1914–18). It was easy to fly and was dependable in **combat**. The airplane had two machine guns that fired through the propellers. The engine gave the *Albatros* a maximum speed of 115 miles (185 km) per hour. It also could fly at an **altitude** of more than 20,000 feet (6,096 m). The wings had the German cross painted on the top. Many **aces** flew the *Albatros*. Manfred von Richthofen was an ace who flew a red *Albatros*. He was known as the Red Baron because of the color of his airplane. The Red Baron won 80 battles before he was shot down in April 1918.

1

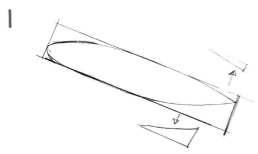

Draw a <u>rectangle</u> at an angle. Next, draw an <u>oval</u> shape inside the rectangle. Notice the triangular shapes that are formed between the oval and the rectangle.

2

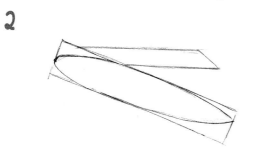

Next, draw two <u>horizontal</u> lines off of the rectangle. These lines are <u>parallel</u>. Connect the lines.

3

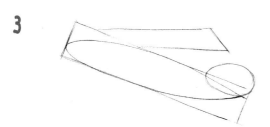

Draw a small oval shape at the end of the rectangle. This is the rudder. Notice how part of the small oval goes into the the larger oval that makes the body of the airplane.

4

Make a <u>semicircle</u> at the center of the plane. Add a triangle below the oval of the rudder. Draw a straight line between these shapes.

5

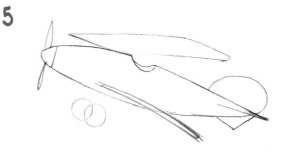

Add two thin oval shapes at the tip of the plane. Draw in the nose of the plane by adding a line. Next, add the bottom wing by drawing two curved lines close together. Then add the wheels by drawing two circles.

6

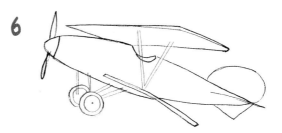

Form the **braces** that hold up the top wing by drawing two sets of lines in a V-shape from the lines of the bottom wing. Draw four more sets of lines from the wheels to the body. To add detail to the wheels, draw a circle inside each of the larger circles.

7

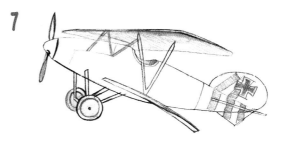

<u>Shade</u> the propeller, the wheels, the pilot's seat, and the underside of the wing. Now you can add more braces to the wing and the stripes and German cross to the tail. Clean up your drawing by erasing extra lines.

The Spirit of St. Louis

In 1927, there was a very brave pilot named Charles Lindbergh. He made the first nonstop flight from New York to Paris. The plane that he flew was called the *Spirit of St. Louis*. The *Spirit of St. Louis* was specially designed for this trip. Its smooth surfaces helped it glide through the sky. Lindbergh chose an engine called the Whirlwind because it was known to be strong. The fuel tanks were located in the wings and behind the engine. It took 33 hours and 30 minutes to make the flight. It also took a lot of physical energy to fly through the difficult weather conditions. Lindbergh had to stay awake and alert for almost two days straight! On May 21, 1927, he landed the plane safely at Le Bourget Field near Paris, France.

1

First draw the body inside a rectangle. Notice how the curved lines at one end of the body meet to become a point.

2

Add the rudder by drawing an upside-down U-shape from the bottom of the body to the top. Notice that this shape is in the left corner of the rectangle.

3

Next, draw a line above the rectangle. Add the wing by drawing two lines at a <u>tilted angle</u> off of the body of the airplane.

4

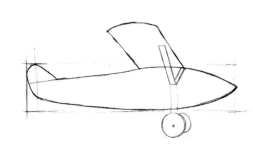

Add one of the braces by drawing a V-shape below the wing. Draw one circle and part of another circle to shape the wheels.

5

Draw the second brace by adding two parallel lines from the middle of the wing to the bottom of the body. Next, add the propeller at the nose of the plane. For detail, add a smaller circle and a semicircle inside the two shapes of the wheels.

6

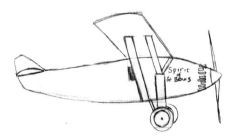

Now, to add the tail wing, draw a semicircle below the curved line that makes the rudder. Then add tiny rectangles to the tip of the airplane to form the engine. Next, add the words *Spirit of St. Louis*. Clean up the drawing by erasing any extra lines.

The Messerschmitt Me-109

In 1935, Professor Willy Messerschmitt of Germany designed the *Messerschmitt Me-109*. The plane was made entirely out of metal. The engine allowed the plane to travel at 385 miles (620 km) per hour. The *Messerschmitt* had two wheels for landing that folded up into the airplane. The wings were attached without braces. The *Messerschmitt* was flown during the Spanish Civil War (1936–39) and World War II (1939–45). It was used in combat because it could carry two machine guns, a cannon, and two more guns under its wings! The weapons made it heavy and clumsy, though. Although it would often lose in combat in the air, it was very successful at bombing its land targets.

1

Draw the body of the airplane
in a tilted, or slanted, rectangle.

2

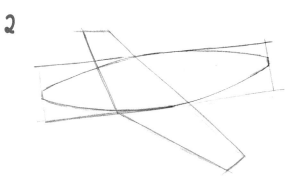

For the wings, draw a triangular shape (with
two flat corners) across the body. The
triangle's top is at the bottom of the body.

3

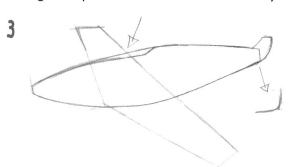

To draw the pilot's window, curve the top line
of the body inward. For the rudder, make the
lines of the body into a curved backward "L".

4

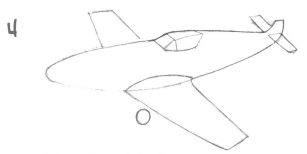

Round the edges of the front wing. Erase extra
lines. Draw the pilot's window. Add a circle for
the wheel and two lines for the tail wings.

5

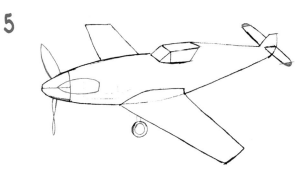

Draw a curved line to form the nose. Then
draw the three blades of the propeller.
Notice how these are oval shapes. Round off
the edges of the tail wings. Draw a smaller
circle in the circle of the wheel.

6

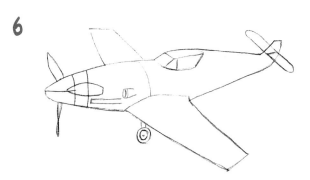

To form the engine, add lines to the front of
the airplane as shown.

7

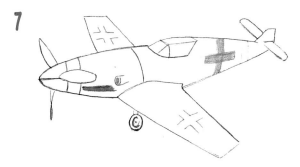

Next, draw the cross design on the wings
and the tail. Clean up the drawing by
erasing any extra lines.

The Douglas DC-3

The *Douglas DC-3* was made in 1936 by the Douglas Aircraft Company of the United States. The *DC-3* is a passenger plane, and most passenger planes at the time were small and slow. They could carry only 10 people and travel at only 160 miles (257 km) per hour. The Douglas Aircraft Company wanted to make a plane that was bigger, more comfortable, faster, and cheaper. The *DC-3* could carry 21 passengers and travel at about 185 miles (298 km) per hour. The cockpit had an **autopilot**, a set of instruments for the pilot, and another for the co-pilot. The sturdy landing gear allowed it to land on short, rough landing strips. The tail carried luggage or **cargo**. Military versions of the *DC-3* carried soldiers.

1

Draw a rectangle at a tilted angle. Inside the rectangle, add an oval shape to form the body of the plane. Make one end of the oval pointed.

2

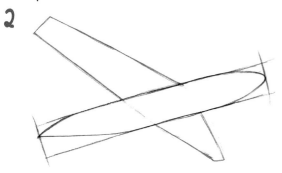

To add the wings, draw two triangular shapes, but with flat tops. Make these two shapes go out from the oval. Make the front wing at the top of the oval much longer than the back one.

3

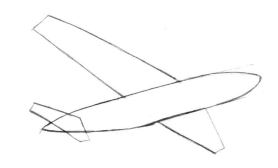

Now add the tail wings by making another triangular shape. Notice that the triangular shape is near the pointed end of the oval.

4

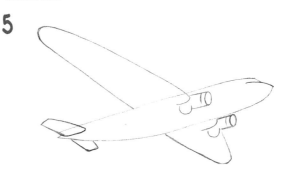

Draw curved lines to shape the nose, wings, and window near the top, front of the airplane. Curve the tail wing where it attaches.

5

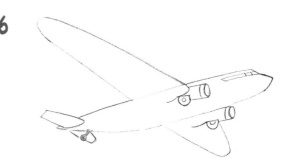

Next, draw the engines by making two small ovals. Draw these ovals near the two wings but not touching them. Then, draw two parallel lines from each oval. Add a semicircle below each of the bottom lines to form the wheels.

6

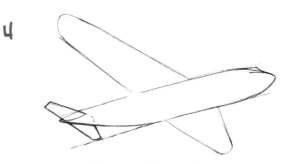

Now draw a smaller circle inside the semicircle of each wheel. Add another wheel below the tail by drawing another circle. Draw two lines in the shape of a hook to connect the tail wheel to the body of the airplane. Next, add the pilots' windows. To finish up the drawing, add some shading and erase any extra lines.

The Mustang P-51

The *Mustang P-51* was a military plane built in 1940. Fighter pilots flew the *Mustang* during World War II (1939–45). The *Mustang* was designed specifically for this war by the government of Great Britain. There was a great need to make a new, faster fighter plane. The Royal Air Force (RAF) designed, built, and flew the *Mustang* in only four months. It usually took a year to design a plane and get it into the air. The *Mustang* could fly at 440 miles (708 km) per hour. The pilot of the airplane was protected by a teardrop-shaped piece of glass. After World War II, the United States Air Force used the *Mustang* until the 1970s.

1

Draw a long and narrow rectangle. Next, draw an oval inside the rectangle to form the shape of the body of the airplane. Make one end pointed and the other end rounded.

2

Draw the pilot's window by making a curved shape in the center of the oval. Notice how the shape looks like a closed mouth. Draw the rudder by making the lines of the body into the shape of a curved backward "L".

3

Next, add the wings by drawing two rectangular shapes on both sides of the plane. Notice that the rectangular shape in the back is much shorter than the other.

4

Draw a rectangular shape on the right at the back of the plane to make the tail wings. (Three short lines at the top and three longer lines at the bottom.)

5

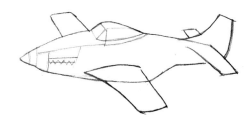

Add some curved lines around the nose of the plane. Next, add a few lines to shape the engine, and four lines to make the pilot's window. Then add two lines to give detail to the tail and tail wing.

6

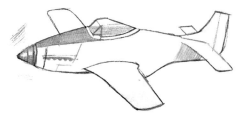

Shade, or fill in, the nose, engine, and the pilot's window. To make the propellers look like they are moving, shade the area above and below the nose. Next, draw the shadow under the tail wings. Then clean up the drawing by erasing any extra lines.

The Concorde Jet

The *Concorde Jet* is one of the world's fastest airplanes. It can travel up to 1,490 miles (2,398 km) per hour. It can fly across the Atlantic Ocean in three hours instead of eight hours like other planes. A long, sleek shape and four **turbojet** engines allow the jet to travel at **supersonic** speed. The *Concorde* began flying passengers in 1973. Its main cabin can seat 100 passengers. The outside covering of the jet protects it from changes in temperature. The nose of the *Concorde* is lowered during the landing to give the pilot a better view of the landing strip. The nose is raised for supersonic flight. The 84-foot (26-m) wings have engines and fuel tanks that carry 34,000 gallons (128,704 liters) of fuel.

18

1

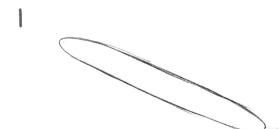

Draw an oval at a sharp angle to form the body of the jet.

2

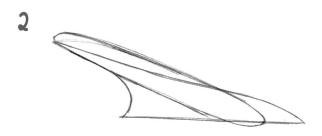

Next, draw a curved triangular shape over the oval. This shape will form the wings of the jet.

3

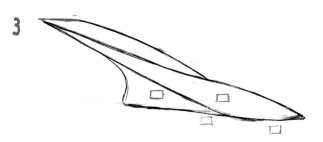

Shape the tip of the airplane by making the end of the oval at the top come to a point. Inside and below the curved triangular shape that forms the wings, draw four boxes. These boxes will begin the shape of the turbojet engines.

4

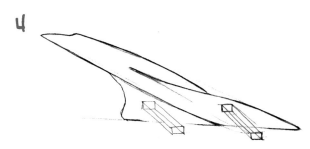

Erase part of the triangular shape near the center of the body to show where the wings begin. Connect the two pairs of boxes with parallel lines to form rectangles. Shape the tip of the plane to form the pilot's window.

5

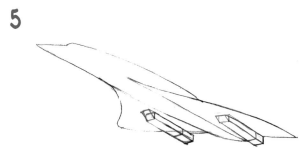

Make the top of the boxes longer by shaping them to form a triangle.

6

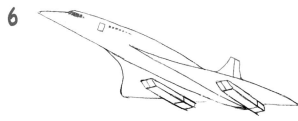

Next, draw the pilot's window and fill it in. For the airplane door, add a small rectangle between the pilot's window and the wings. Then add passenger windows by drawing seven small dots along the body. For the tail, draw three curved lines on top of the wing. Join these lines with a straight line at the top. Erase any extra lines from the drawing.

The B-2 (Stealth) Bomber

Some people say the *B-2 Bomber* looks like an unidentified flying object, or UFO. Its unusual triangular shape makes it appear mysterious. The military uses this plane in combat. It is called a **stealth** bomber because it has a dark coating that keeps it from being seen on **radar**. An airplane that cannot be seen on radar is good for combat. This way it can sneak up on its target. The *B-2 Bomber* has four engines that make it go up to 700 miles (1,127 km) per hour. That is almost 14 times faster than you go in a car. When a plane flies that fast, it is going faster than the speed of sound, or over 1,088 feet (331 m) per second!

1

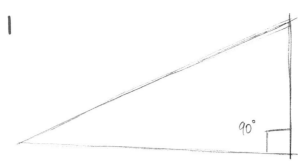

Draw the body of the plane by making a
<u>right triangle</u>.

2

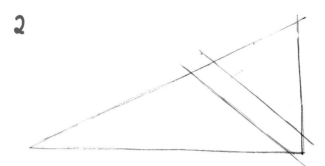

Add two parallel lines that run through the
center of the triangle.

3

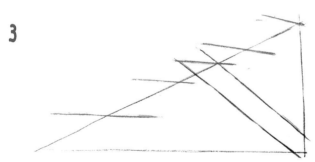

Add five horizontal, parallel lines as shown.
Notice that the lines are not an equal
distance apart.

4

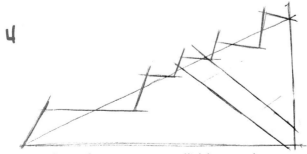

Next, draw five more parallel lines. They
should be vertical to the first set of parallel
lines. These lines will form step-like shapes.

5

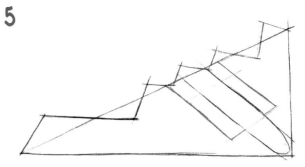

Draw two lines that are parallel to the center
lines drawn in step two. Round off the first
parallel lines to form the tip of the airplane
where the pilot sits.

6

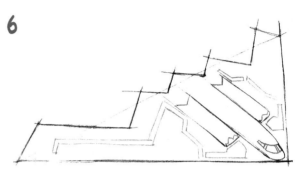

Next, add one V-shape to connect the bottom
set of parallel lines. Add another V-shape to
connect the top set of lines. These shapes
form the engines! Add the windows to the
front of the plane. Then add the design of
long, thin bent rectangles.

7

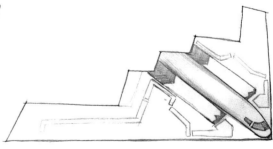

Clean up the drawing by erasing the extra
lines. Shade in the areas as shown.

21

Drawing Terms

These are some words and shapes you will need to know to draw airplanes:

3-D box

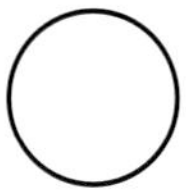

circle

horizontal (across, or level)

oval

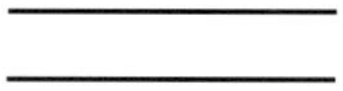

parallel

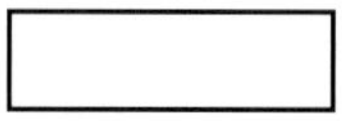

rectangle

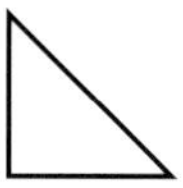

right triangle

semicircle

shade, or shading

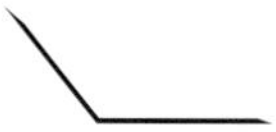

tilted angle

triangle

vertical (up and down)

Glossary

aces (AYS-iz) War pilots who have won more than five air battles.

altitude (AL-tih-tood) The height an airplane flies above sea level.

attitude (AH-tih-tood) A person's outlook or position toward a fact or situation.

autopilot (AW-toh-py-lit) An airplane instrument that steers the plane by itself.

braces (BRAYS-iz) Objects that hold parts up or keep them together.

cargo (KAR-goh) The load of goods carried by an airplane, ship, or truck.

cockpit (KAHK-pit) The space in the airplane where the pilot and co-pilot sit to control the plane.

combat (KAHM-bat) A battle or fight.

elevator (EL-ih-vay-ter) The front panels of an airplane. These panels move up and down to make the plane go up or down.

engine (EN-jin) A machine inside the airplane. It uses fuel to make the airplane move.

nose (NOHZ) The front part of a plane.

patience (PAY-shunts) The ability to wait calmly for something.

persistence (per-SIS-tehns) Continuing to do something without giving up.

propeller (preh-PEL-er) The part of the airplane that spins around and helps move the airplane forward.

radar (RAY-dar) A machine that uses radio waves to find out the location of objects in the air or on the ground.

rudder (RUD-er) A piece of wood or metal attached to the back of an airplane that helps guide the plane in certain directions.

stealth bomber (STELTH BAH-mer) An airplane that cannot be seen on radar.

supersonic (soo-per-SAHN-ik) Moving faster than the speed of sound.

turbojet (TER-bow-jet) A very fast engine that burns a mixture of pressurized air and fuel.

wings (WINGZ) Large pieces of metal or wood that are on opposite sides of an airplane's body. They help the plane stay up and fly through the air.

Index

Web Sites

To learn more about airplanes, check out these Web sites:

http://www.yahoo.com/planes.com
http://www.concorde.cybair.com/